Mr. Tuck and the 13 Heroes

John Harris, Author

Sophie Harris, Illustrator

Regeneration Writers Press, LLC

Macon, Georgia

Published in 2016 by Regeneration Writers Press, LLC
1177 Adams Street, Macon, GA 31201

regenerationpress.com
editor@regenerationpress.com

ISBN-10:1-945098-90-2
ISBN-13:978-1-945098-90-1

John Harris, Author
Sophie Harris, Illustrator
Colin Harris, Consulting Editor
Margaret Eskew, Publishing Editor
Jerome A. Gratigny, Technical Editor

Order *Mr. Tuck and the 13 Heroes*
from regenerationpress.com
or amazon.com
or Regeneration Writers Press, LLC
1177 Adams Street
Macon, GA 31201-1507

Dedicated to

Shirley and Mike

Partners in Courage and Hope

and to the

Thirteen Heroes and Their Families

Then and Now

Stewards of the Legacy

PRAISE

"Mr. Tuck and the 13 Heroes is a tender children's book about a very difficult time in education. Things are much better now, thanks to educators like Mr. Tuck and the courageous children in this story. We all should continue our journey for meaningful diversity in all areas of education."

Richard W. Riley
Former US Secretary of Education
Former Governor of South Carolina

"Mr. Tuck and the 13 Heroes is a well-told story that beautifully explains a difficult time in our history."

Melinda Long
Award-Winning Children's Book Author
Author of *How I Became a Pirate*

"I had the privilege of hearing this story from Dr. Brooks Tuck himself several years ago, and this book captures the authentic voice of an authentic hero. It tells the story of his humble heroism, his compassionate courage, and his quietly profound influence on the children in his school and on the adults in his community during a very difficult time in our history."

Allison C. Gilmore
Mercer University Professor of Education
Close Colleague of Brooks Tuck

"This true story is a 'must tell' story that should indeed be shared with today's youth who may know very little about any of the pioneers in the desegregation of public education. Those reassuring words Mr. Tuck spoke to the thirteen children that first day they attended Fairview Elementary – 'I'm so glad you are here' – are captured in this book exactly as I recall hearing him say them as he shared this story during his commencement address at Mercer in 2010."

Jacquelyn Culpepper, Ph.D.
Associate Professor of Reading Education
Mercer University

"This book tells the remarkable story of the daunting challenge and the daring courage of all involved in the integration of one small elementary school in Georgia. Its portrayal of the situation is realistic, convincing, and communicative, both through words and illustrations. This is a great book for children and a 'must read' book for everyone."

Karen Becnel Moore
Associate Professor of Spanish
Xavier University of Louisiana

"Unless we have effective and positive models for interracial relationships in our literature, we cannot make substantive progress in the conversation on race. *Mr. Tuck and the 13 Heroes* provides a refreshing and inspiring model that points the direction toward better relations between blacks and whites. In this age of multiracial and multicultural communities, every child and parent should read this book."

Florence A. Lyons
Professor of Speech and Theater
Albany State University (Georgia)

"A powerful story beautifully written and illustrated. This book tells the story of a difficult and often violent period of our history in a way that is accessible and age-appropriate for young children."

Julie Whidden Long
Associate Pastor & Minister of Children and Families
First Baptist Church of Christ
Macon, Georgia

It is hard to believe now, but there was a time in our country's history when white children and black children could not go to school together.

Things started to change for the better in 1954, when the Supreme Court said that it was against the law to separate the students. Some places took longer than others to start changing.

Henry County in Georgia was one of those places. In 1966, the court finally ordered Henry County to integrate -- to let black children and white children go to the same school.

Many people in Henry County did not like this. Since they had to do it, they decided to let it happen in just one school.

That school was going to be Fairview
Elementary. A man named Mr. Tuck
was the principal.

Before Mr. Tuck came to Fairview, it was the school that was in the worst shape of all the white schools in the county.

Mr. Tuck wanted to change that.

He and his wife did a lot of work to make it look better. They even put new paint on the walls themselves.

Under Mr. Tuck's leadership, Fairview became a very good school.

Mr. Tuck believed that all children should be able to go to a good school.

When the county needed one school to let the children attend, Mr. Tuck quickly volunteered Fairview.

This made many white people in the
Fairview area very mad, and they did
some mean things to Mr. Tuck's family.

They called his house and said terrible things. They painted mean words on the road outside his house.

They tried to scare the family by saying that there was a bomb in their car. They even threatened to hurt Mr. Tuck's son, Mike.

All of this was very difficult for Mr. Tuck
and his family, but he knew he was doing
the right thing.

When black families were given the
chance to send their students to Fairview,
only a few families responded -- thirteen
children in all.

The school that the black children attended was in terrible shape. The books were old and missing pages, the desks were broken, and the building was falling apart.

The families of the thirteen children
wanted their sons and daughters to have
something better -- even though they knew
that changing schools would be very hard
for them.

The weeks leading up to the first day of school were very difficult. There were lots of loud, mean-spirited protests.

The biggest protest was on the first day of school itself.

Early that morning, hundreds of people lined the sidewalk at the school.

When the bus carrying the thirteen black children arrived, the children could hear and see the people shouting at them. A few people had guns and ropes -- holding them up to intimidate the children.

The children were so scared.

As they looked over the crowd toward the school, they could see a man step through the front door.

Many of the students recognized the man as Mr. Tuck, the white man who they had heard was going to be their principal.

The crowd insulted and threatened Mr. Tuck as he walked toward the bus.

Mr. Tuck stepped onto the bus and spoke to the frightened children.

"Boys and girls," he said, "this is your school. I am Mr. Tuck, your principal."

"We are going to get through this together," he said. "I'm so glad you are here."

Mr. Tuck took the hand of one of the girls up front. The two of them stepped off the bus and walked hand in hand up the walk toward the school.

Once the little girl was safely inside the building, Mr. Tuck stepped back outside, locked the door behind him, and went back toward the bus.

Mr. Tuck made thirteen trips to the bus that morning. He held the hands of the students, and he even carried some of the smaller ones.

The children arrived safely to school, and Fairview Elementary was integrated -- at long last.

The next few weeks and months were still very hard for Mr. Tuck and the thirteen children, but things did get better gradually.

Years later when Mr. Tuck was asked about his experiences that day, he said, "This is not my story. This is the children's story. They were the real heroes that day."

Many years after that memorable morning, Mr. Tuck became sick and had to go to the hospital. He did get better, but he had to stay there for a while.

He drifted in and out of sleep frequently during his stay in the hospital. He was not aware of much, but he could tell that there were many doctors and visitors coming and going.

As the days went on, he noticed that there was a particular nurse named Melinda who was in the room a lot -- sometimes during the day

and sometimes late at night.

"You are in here all the time," he said to the nurse. "I've got plenty of people here to take care of me. You should go home and get some rest."

Melinda smiled. "Mr. Tuck, you don't recognize me, but I sure do know you."

"You held my hand and walked with me to my first day at Fairview Elementary. You didn't leave me on that day, and I'm not leaving you."

"We'll get through this together," she said.

Mr. Tuck smiled at her and said, "I'm so glad you are here."

Dr. Curtis Brooks Tuck

(1938-2012)

Brooks Tuck was an educator for fifty years, as a teacher and principal in the Henry County and Dekalb County schools, and as a teacher with Mercer University in Atlanta. A native of Gwinnett County, Georgia, he was a graduate of Mercer University, with graduate degrees from the University of Georgia.

From his courageous role early in his career as a pioneer in the desegregation of public education, to his wise counsel and supervision of student teachers late in his career, Brooks Tuck was a consummate teacher with a vision of what can be for each student and the practical wisdom to help bring it about. His wife Shirley and son Mike were indispensible partners in his work throughout his career.

In 2010, Mercer University conferred on Brooks Tuck the Doctor of Humanities degree, in recognition of his life of service to education. In his commencement address that day, he told for the first time publicly the story of the thirteen heroes.

Three generations of our family have been profoundly influenced by the life and legacy of Brooks Tuck. I am grateful that my son and granddaughter have used their gifts to preserve his story.

Writer John Harris is Professor of Mathematics at Furman University. Illustrator Sophie Harris is an art major at Furman.

This book is intended to ensure that this story will continue to be told.

Colin Harris
Professor Emeritus of Religious Studies
Mercer University
June 2016